D1071566

By Gregory Vogt

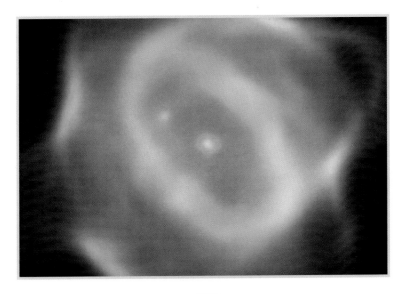

Raintree Steck-Vaughn Publishers

A Harcourt Company

Austin · New York
www.steck-vaughn.com

OUR UNIVERSE

Published by Raintree Steck-Vaughn Publishers,
an imprint of Steck-Vaughn Company.

Library of Congress Cataloging-in-Publication Data
Vogt, Gregory.
    Nebulas/by Gregory Vogt.
        p.cm.--(Our universe)
    Includes index.
    ISBN 0-7398-3108-9
    1. Nebulae--Juvenile literature. [1. Nebulae. 2. Stars.] I. Title.
QB855.2 .V64 2000
523.1'135--dc21

00-33817

Printed in the United States of America
10 9 8 7 6 5 4 3 2 1 W 02 01 00

Produced by Compass Books

Photo Acknowledgments
Matt Bobrowsky (Orbital Sciences Corporation) and NASA, title page; NASA, cover, 10; Hubble Heritage Team (NASA/AURA/STScI), 14, 18, 22, 24, 30, 38; Wolfgang Brandner (JPL/IPAC), Eva K. Grebel (University of Washington), You-Hua Chu (University of Illinois, Urbana-Champaign) and NASA, 6; J. Hester and P. Scowen (AZ State Univ.), NASA; T.A.Rector, B.Wolpa, M.Hanna, KPNO 0.9-m Mosaic, AURA/NOAO/NSF, 13; ESO, 16; N.A.Sharp/AURA/NOAO/NSF, 17; J.P. Harrington and K.J. Borkowski (University of Maryland), and NASA, 20; R. Sahai and J. Trauger (JPL), the WFPC2 Science Team and NASA, 27, 28; C.R. O'Dell and S.K. Wong (Rice Univ.), NASA, 35; SOHO, 36; Jeff Hester and Paul Scowen (Arizona State University) and NASA, 41; NASA and B. Reipurth (CASA, Univ. of Colorado), 32-33; C. Burrows (ESA/STScI), HST, NASA, 42; H. Bond (ST ScI) and NASA, 44

Content Consultant
David Jewitt
Professor of Astronomy
University of Hawaii Institute for Astronomy

Contents

4/3/02 gift

Diagram of a Nebula

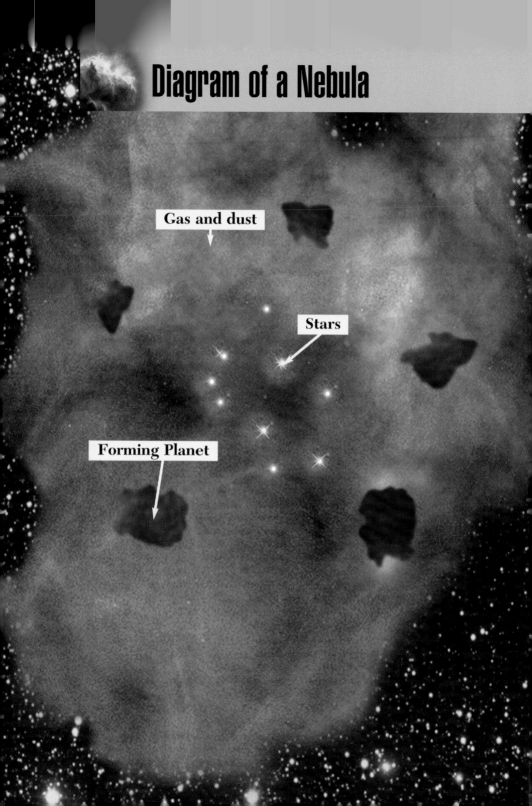

Gas and dust

Stars

Forming Planet

A Quick Look at Nebulas

What are nebulas?
Nebulas are clouds of gas and dust in space.

What are nebulas made of?
Nebulas are mostly made of hydrogen gas. They can also
be made of helium, oxygen, and nitrogen. Different
nebulas have different kinds of gas in them.

What do nebulas look like?
Nebulas can be many different colors and shapes. Some
look like clouds. Others have towers of gas. Still others
have ringlike or hourglass shapes.

How do nebulas get their names?
Nebulas are often nicknamed after the shapes they
remind people of. For example, the nebula on the title
page is nicknamed the Stingray Nebula.

This nebula is called NGC 3603. It contains stars in many different stages of development.

About Nebulas

The universe is made up of planets, stars, and everything that exists in space. Stars are balls of very hot gas that give off light and heat.

Most of the universe is empty space. There are many stars, but they are very far apart from each other. In some places, gas and small pieces of dust float in between the stars. The dust and gas sometimes form clouds called nebulas.

Nebulas are places where stars are born and where stars die. Many stars can be born inside one nebula. Dying stars slowly shed their gases to make new nebulas. Some old stars explode when they die. Their gases mix with dust to make new nebulas.

Nebulas can reflect the light of nearby stars. Sometimes heat from stars nearby or inside them makes their gases glow. Some nebulas block light. These nebulas are dark.

How Big Are Nebulas?

Nebulas range in size from millions of miles to dozens of light-years across. A light-year is used to measure the huge distances between objects in space. It is the distance light travels in one year, or 6 trillion miles (9.6 trillion km). A nebula 60 trillion miles (97 trillion km) wide is 10 light-years across.

Gas and Dust

Nebulas are partly made of gases. Hydrogen is the main gas in nebulas. Nebulas may also contain oxygen, helium, and nitrogen. These are the main gases in Earth's air. But there is not enough oxygen in nebulas for people to breathe. A person would have to take 10 million breaths in a nebula to replace one breath on Earth.

The dust in nebulas is made up of very small, solid particles. One piece of dust is 25 times smaller than a period on this page. People cannot see the individual particles, only the clusters of dust particles in nebulas.

Nebula dust can be made of many things. The dust grains can be carbon, iron, calcium, or sodium. They may be made up of rocky materials. Dust grains also may have coatings of ice.

New stars are forming in the thick gas towers of this nebula.

Astronauts are repairing the Hubble Space Telescope.

Telescopes

Astronomers use many tools to study nebulas. Astronomers are scientists who study objects in space. The most important tools are telescopes. Telescopes make faraway objects look clearer and closer. Most astronomers use electronic cameras on the telescopes to take pictures. Astronomers study the pictures on their computers.

Astronomers can see many nebulas through telescopes. These nebulas are bright and easy for astronomers to spot. Others are dark and hard to see.

There are several kinds of telescopes. A refracting telescope uses lenses to collect and focus light. A reflecting telescope uses mirrors to collect and focus light. Radio telescopes collect radio waves instead of light. This telescope uses a curved radio antenna to catch radio waves from space.

Space telescopes are on spacecraft that orbit around Earth. These telescopes can see farther and take clearer pictures because they are above Earth's atmosphere. The Hubble Space Telescope is a very powerful space telescope. It is the best telescope for studying faraway objects in space. Scientists on Earth use radio signals to control the Hubble. The telescope radios its pictures back to Earth.

Emission Nebulas

There are three kinds of nebulas. The first kind is the emission nebula. These nebulas glow and give off their own light.

Emission nebulas are like neon signs. A neon sign is made from a bent glass tube full of neon gas. Neon gas is very thin. Electricity flows through the gas when the sign is turned on. The electricity makes the gas glow.

The gases in emission nebulas glow, too. Emission nebulas often have many new stars forming in them. The energy from the hot new stars inside the nebulas makes the gases glow. These stars are about 30,000° Fahrenheit (16,650° C). This is about 60 times hotter than a kitchen oven.

Light from the stars heats up the nebula's gases. The gases begin to glow. Each kind of gas in an emission nebula glows a different color. Gases can glow in many different colors, such as red, pink, green, or orange.

The Rosette Nebula is 3,000 light-years away from Earth. In this picture, its hydrogen gas is red. Oxygen is green, and sulfur is blue.

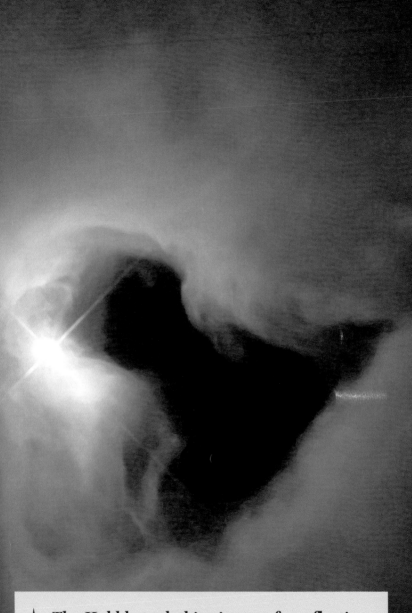

The Hubble took this picture of a reflection
nebula in the constellation Orion.

Reflection Nebulas

Reflection nebulas are the second kind of nebulas. The gases in these nebulas are not hot enough to glow. Instead, reflection nebulas only reflect the light of stars nearby or inside them.

Reflection nebulas have cool or medium-hot stars inside them. Average stars are only about 10,000° Fahrenheit (5,540° C). Other stars are even cooler. The heat energy from these stars is not enough to cause nebula gas to glow.

Reflection nebulas appear to glow. But they really reflect light. The light from nearby stars bounces off the dust in reflection nebulas. Astronomers can see this reflected light, even though the gases do not glow.

Light from stars is many different colors. Starlight contains red, orange, yellow, green, blue, violet-blue, and violet light. The colors mix together to make the white light people see on Earth.

Most colors of light scatter. Some colors scatter more than other colors. For example, red light easily passes straight through nebula dust. The dust does not reflect it. But blue light scatters. It bounces off the dust particles. The dust reflects the blue light. This gives most reflection nebulas their blue color.

Dark nebulas like this one (left) block light. The Horsehead Nebula is a dark nebula made of thick dust (right).

Dark Nebulas

Dark nebulas are the third kind of nebula. These thick clouds of gas and dust appear black. They look like giant shadows in space.

There are no stars inside or near dark nebulas. They are black because they have no hot stars inside to make their gas glow. And they do not have stars close enough to bounce light off their dust. Dark nebulas even block the light of distant stars behind them. This makes dark nebulas look like holes in space.

Horsehead Nebula

The Horsehead Nebula is a dark nebula. It is shaped like a horse's head. Astronomers can see it because its shape blocks the light from other nebulas in that part of the sky.

The Horsehead Nebula is in the middle of the Orion constellation. A constellation is a group of stars. Ancient peoples and astronomers have grouped the stars in patterns that people can remember. They decided what these star patterns looked like. Orion is a group of stars. The stars' pattern reminded people of a hunter called Orion in Greek stories.

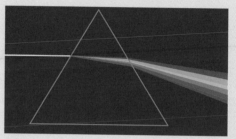

Spectroscopes

Astronomers use tools called spectroscopes to study light. Some spectroscopes are made of material with many tiny grooves. The grooves separate white light into all the different colors of light. Other spectroscopes have prisms. Prisms are triangle-shaped pieces of glass that separate light.

This photograph shows the colorful gas swirls of the large Carina Nebula and the smaller Keyhole Nebula. Scientists study the colors of a nebula.

Studying Light

Light is very useful to astronomers. Light shows astronomers the shapes of faraway objects. The strength and amount of light shows astronomers how big objects are. They can also tell how hot a star is from its light. The hottest stars are blue. Medium temperature stars are yellow and white. Cooler stars are red. The change in a star's light tells astronomers where the star is moving.

Light also shows what elements make up a nebula. Elements are pure materials found in nature. Elements include gases like hydrogen and helium, metals like iron, and minerals like calcium and sulfur. The universe contains many different elements. Elements give off light when they are heated. Each element gives off its own special set of colors.

Astronomers study the colors in emission nebulas. The colors from different elements blend together. Astronomers use a special instrument called a spectroscope to study the light. The spectroscope separates the colors. Then astronomers can tell which elements made them and figure out what makes up the nebula. This helps astronomers learn more about nebulas and how stars form.

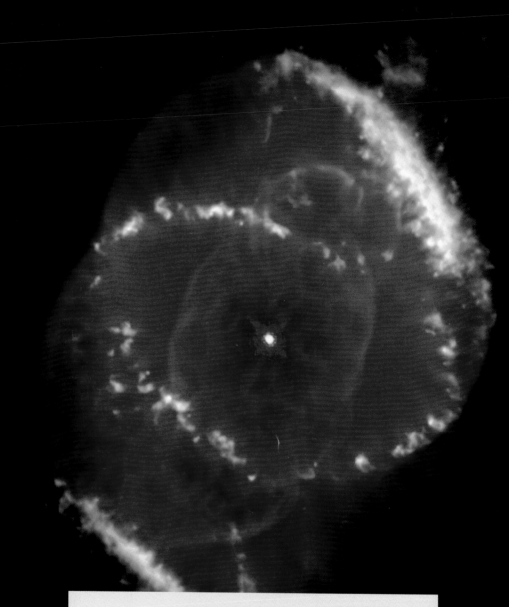

Colorful shell-like layers of gas surround a small star in the Cat's Eye Nebula.

Planetary Nebulas

Looking for planets is part of an astronomer's job. Our solar system has nine known planets. Some astronomers think our solar system might have even more planets that have not yet been discovered.

Telescopes in the past were not as powerful as telescopes are today. Long ago, astronomers looked through weak telescopes. They found small round objects that looked like planets.

Later, scientists made more powerful telescopes. Astronomers used the new telescopes to study the round objects. They discovered that the objects were nebulas and not planets. Astronomers named these planetary nebulas because they look round like planets.

Today, the Hubble Space Telescope is helping scientists find new nebulas. Scientists study detailed pictures from the Hubble to learn more about nebulas.

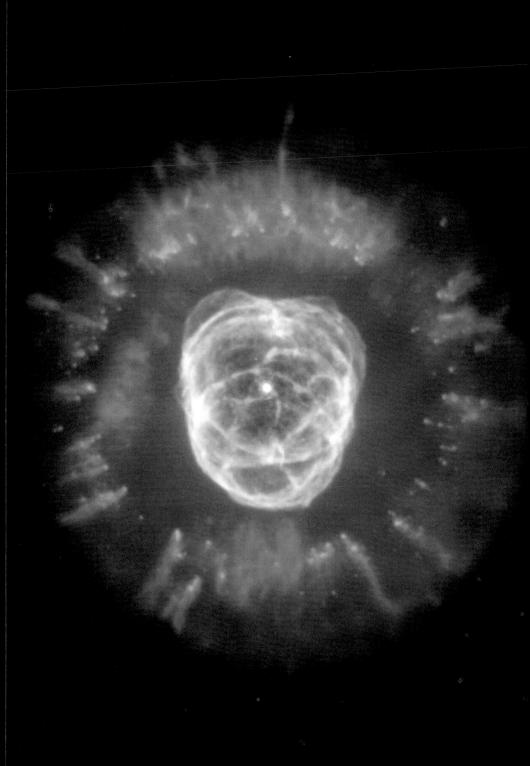

How Planetary Nebulas Form

Planetary nebulas form during the final stages of some stars' lives. A dying star releases the hot gases in its outer layers. The gases remain drifting around the dying star. They keep their ringlike shape as they slowly float away in space. A star may shed many rings of gas. Each ring looks like a shell around the star.

At first, the rings of gas are still hot from the star. They are hot enough to glow. Slowly, the gases cool off. They stop glowing and drift away into space.

After time, the star burns up all of its gases. Then it stops releasing rings of gas. It cools off and dies. A dead star is called a black dwarf.

Astronomers believe there are about 10,000 planetary nebulas in our galaxy. These nebulas will last about 25,000 years. It will take thousands of years for the gas and dust to slowly separate and drift into space.

This planetary nebula is nicknamed the Eskimo Nebula. A white dwarf star glows in its center.

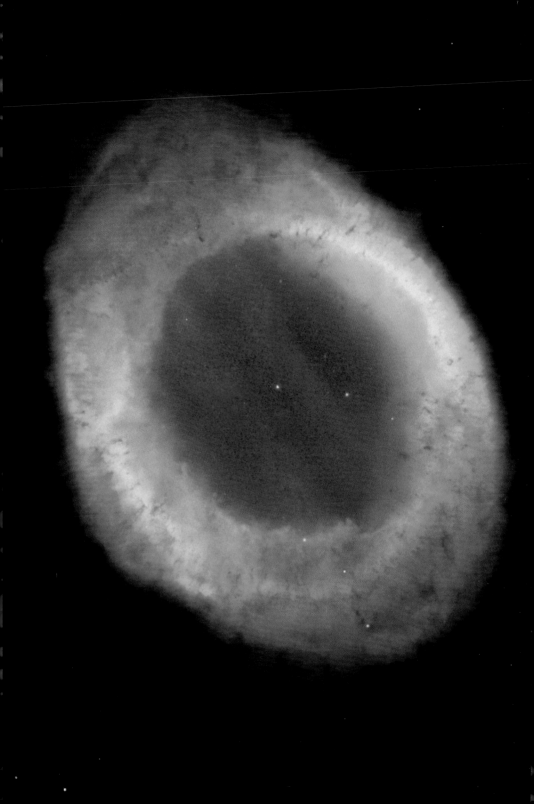

The Ring Nebula

The Ring Nebula was the first planetary nebula discovered. A French astronomer spotted the nebula 200 years ago in the constellation Lyra. The Ring Nebula is about 2,000 light-years away from Earth. It is about one light-year wide.

The Ring Nebula looks like a large, shining seashell. It has a bright, dying star in its center. A ring of glowing, colored gases surrounds the star.

The star in its center was once bigger than our Sun. It exploded and blew out its outer gas layers into space. The ring grew larger as the gas traveled outward from the star and into space.

The explosion turned the star into a white dwarf star about the size of Earth. A white dwarf is one type of small, dying star. The dwarf star in the Ring Nebula still creates enough energy to heat the nebula's gases. This makes them glow.

In the photograph on page 24, the outer red ring is nitrogen. This is the coolest ring of gas. The green is oxygen. The blue is very hot helium.

 The Ring Nebula is about one light-year across.

25

Hourglass Nebula

The Hourglass Nebula is a planetary nebula in the Milky Way galaxy. The Milky Way is a huge group of stars and planets that includes our solar system. The Hourglass Nebula is about 8,000 light-years from Earth.

The Hourglass Nebula has a strange appearance. It has a blue-green oval that looks like an eye in its center. Orange and red rings are on the top and bottom. This makes the nebula look like an hourglass or figure 8 in pictures.

Scientists are not sure why the Hourglass Nebula has its unusual shape. One idea is that the star at the center of the nebula blew away many large layers of gases. This happened a long time ago. The star continues to blow away gas particles. The fast-moving particles are striking the slower-moving layers of gas. They pushed the gas layers into the hourglass shape.

There are three main kinds of gas in the Hourglass Nebula. Each gas glows a different color. In the picture on page 27, nitrogen is red. Hydrogen is green, and oxygen is blue.

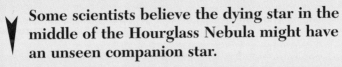
Some scientists believe the dying star in the middle of the Hourglass Nebula might have an unseen companion star.

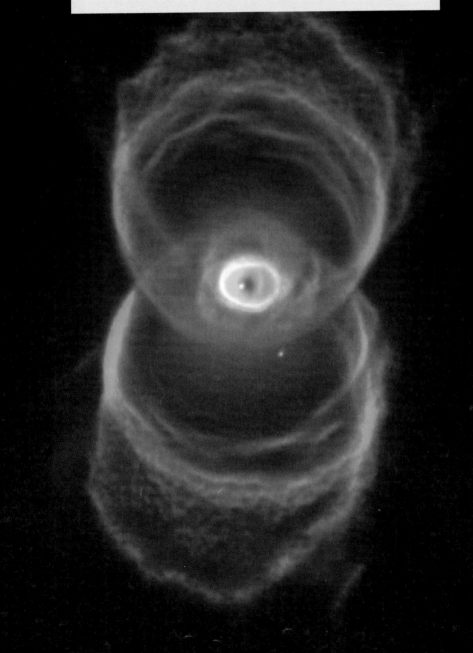

Egg Nebula

The Egg Nebula is a planetary nebula 3,000 light-years away from Earth. Astronomers named it the Egg Nebula because they thought it looked like an egg. This nebula is larger than our entire solar system.

The star that made the nebula was once a giant star that blew away its outer gas layers. Now it is a white dwarf star. The gases from the exploding star are moving outward into space at 115,000 miles (185,000 km) per hour. The gases formed the nebula.

Astronomers have a hard time seeing the white dwarf star. A thick cloud of dust blocks its view. The star in the center of the Egg Nebula also has many blown-out shells of gas surrounding it.

The Egg Nebula looks like searchlights are streaming from it. Some astronomers think light from the star makes the searchlight beams. The light streams through holes in the nebula's gas layers like sunlight streams through dark clouds on Earth.

A thick cloud of dust hides the star in the middle of the Egg Nebula.

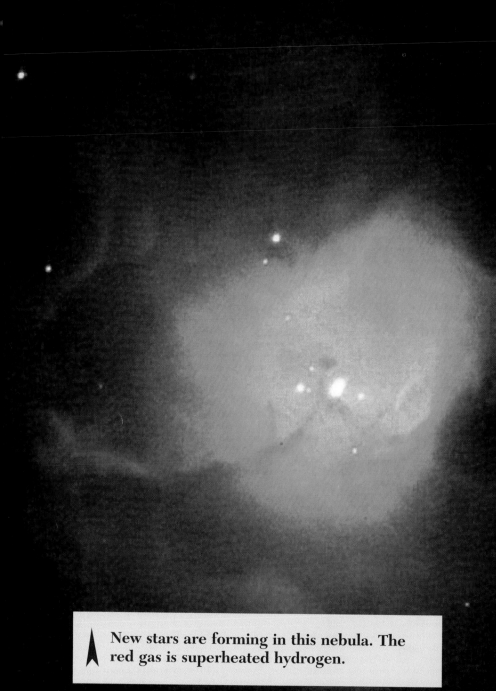

New stars are forming in this nebula. The red gas is superheated hydrogen.

Stars Are Born

The gases to form stars come from nebulas. But something has to happen to the gases before stars can form. Sometimes nearby stars explode. The explosions send shock waves into space. These powerful currents of energy pack the gas and dust in nebulas close together. The cloud gets smaller and hotter as the gas and dust move closer together. A large clump forms.

Eventually, the center of the clump becomes hot enough for nuclear fusion to begin. The gravity and heat in the clump push particles of hydrogen gas together. The particles are squeezed so tightly that they stick together. Two hydrogen gas atoms make one helium atom when they stick together. Energy in the form of light and heat is released when the atoms stick together. A star is born once this process begins.

The gas jet streaming from this new star is 12 light-years long.

Jets

The creation of a new star from a nebula is a powerful event. At times, some of the gases falling into the star are thrown back out into space.

These powerful jets of gas shoot outward from the star's poles. The poles are the most northern and southern parts of an object in space. The jets stream into space. They plow through the nebula that surrounds the star.

The gases in the jets are so hot that they glow. The hot gas jets create enough energy to make the gases in the nebula glow, too. So the nebula's gases begin to glow as soon as the jets hit them.

Sometimes, the jets shoot out like bullets. The bullets of gas travel 500,000 miles (800,000 km) per hour. That is fast enough to travel from the Sun to Earth in just one week. The jets stretch out from the new star for hundreds of billions of miles.

Great Orion Nebula

During winter, people on Earth can see the constellation of Orion in the night sky. Some of the stars in this constellation look like a sword. A nebula is in the middle of the sword. It is called the Great Orion Nebula. It is 20 light-years wide and 1,500 light-years from Earth.

The Great Orion Nebula is the closest star-forming area to Earth. Many stars are being born in the Great Orion Nebula. The center of the nebula is very bright. The light comes from four very hot, young stars. Astronomers have counted 700 other young stars there too. The stars are all in different stages of growth.

Some of the new stars are shooting jets of gas into space. The jets send waves rushing through the nebula. The waves travel at speeds of 100,000 miles (160,000 km) per hour. At that speed, a person could travel around the Earth four times in one second.

This image shows a small area near the center of the Great Orion Nebula. New stars send jets of gas streaming through the nebula.

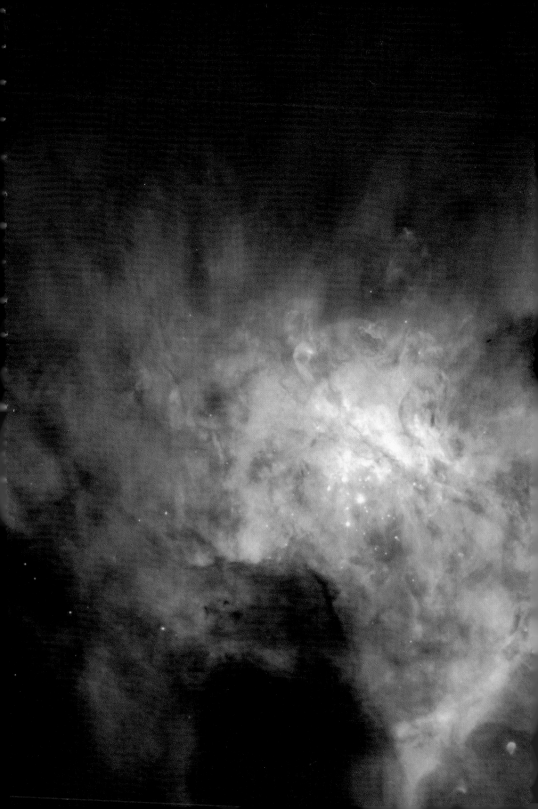

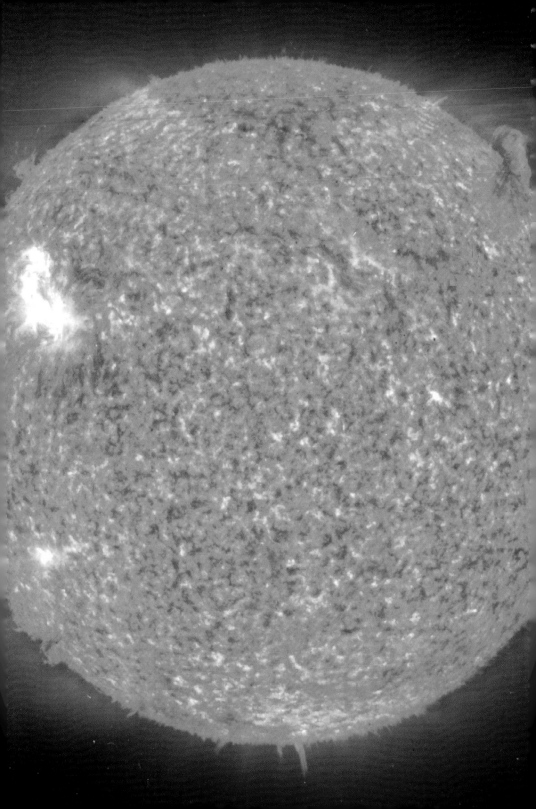

Planets Form

The Great Orion Nebula is a place of much activity. Astronomers have counted more than 150 spinning disks of gas and dust in the nebula. The disks are turning like pinwheels.

Astronomers think the disks may be the start of new solar systems. Our solar system formed when the Sun was created. The planets and moons were made from leftover gas and dust.

The Sun started to form inside a nebula. Most of the nebula's gas and dust began falling to the center. Gravity squeezed it together. The large clump that became the Sun formed and grew larger over thousands of years. Then it got very hot and became bright.

The remaining cloud of dust continued to spin. Small clumps began to form. They grew larger and larger until they became planets. The planets continued the spinning motion and orbited the Sun.

Scientists believe the disks in the Great Orion Nebula will become stars and planets too. Some of these disks are very large. They may become solar systems with many planets like our solar system.

The Sun is the closest star to Earth. Billions of years ago, it formed inside a nebula.

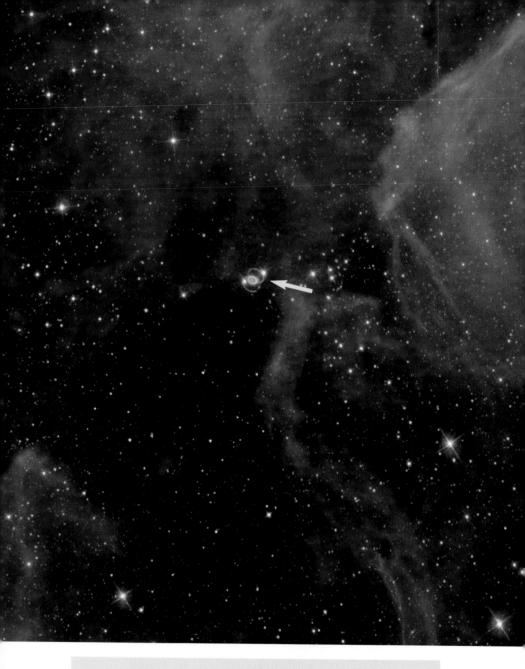

A distant exploding star has thrown off rings of gas.

Stars Die

Stars can be different sizes. Small stars like our Sun die slowly. They shrink and burn up all their hydrogen. They become planetary nebulas as they slowly shed layers of gas into space. Large, heavy stars explode all at once. An exploding star is called a supernova. It can be brighter than the light from billions of stars.

The core of a large star shrinks until it caves in. This creates an explosion of shock waves that race outward, blowing fragments of the star into space. The fragments shoot away at speeds of 25,000 miles (40,000 km) per second. Exploded gas from the supernova forms a new nebula. The gas remains hot and glows for many years.

Crab Nebula

In the year A.D. 1054, Chinese astronomers were watching the sky. They saw a new star suddenly appear. The star flashed brightly. People could see it even during the day. After a few months, the star faded and was never seen again.

Pueblo Indians of New Mexico also saw the exploding star. One of their artists painted a picture of it under a rock cliff. The picture shows a 10-point star.

The Chinese and the Pueblo were observing the destruction of a star. They saw a supernova. For a time, the supernova glowed brighter than millions of stars combined.

The supernova was 6,000 light-years away. It took 6,000 years for the light from the explosion to reach Earth. So, the Chinese were watching an explosion that had happened 6,000 years earlier.

Modern astronomers used telescopes to find the place in the sky where the Chinese astronomers saw the supernova. They found a nebula in the constellation of Taurus. The exploding star had made the nebula. Astronomers named it the Crab Nebula because its shape reminded them of a crab.

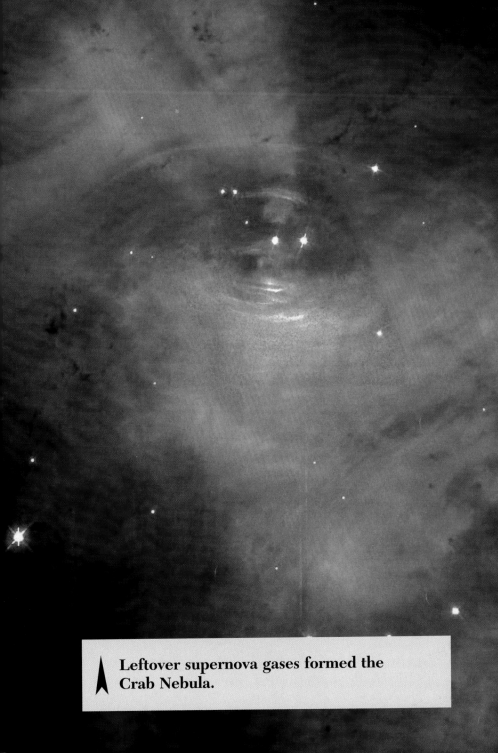

Leftover supernova gases formed the Crab Nebula.

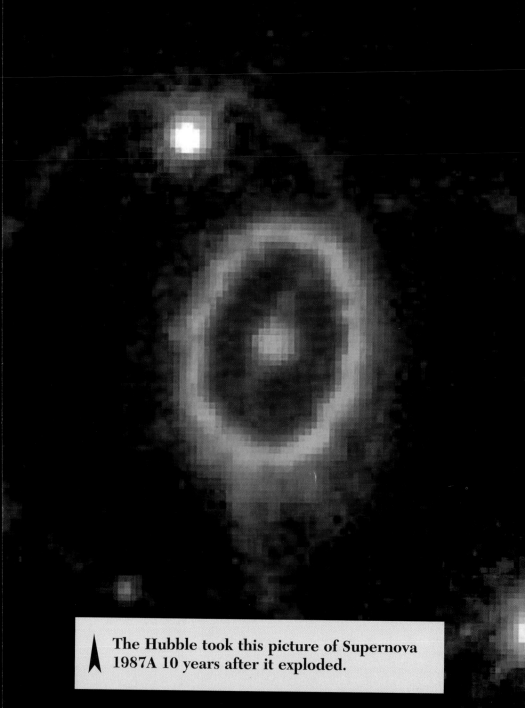

The Hubble took this picture of Supernova 1987A 10 years after it exploded.

Supernova 1987A

In 1987, an astronomer spotted a bright star in a nearby galaxy. The star had not appeared in earlier pictures of the galaxy. The astronomer had discovered a new supernova.

Astronomers named it supernova 1987A because it was the first one discovered in 1987. Many astronomers around the world began to study the exploding star. The supernova was many light-years away. It took 167,000 years for light from the supernova explosion to travel to Earth. So, they were watching a supernova that had exploded long ago.

Astronomers believe the supernova was actually a double star. One star was large, and one was small. Long ago, the two stars crashed into each other. The crash destroyed the small star. Its gas formed a ring nebula around the larger star.

Later, the larger star exploded. Energy from the explosion lit up the ring. It became bright enough for astronomers on Earth to see it.

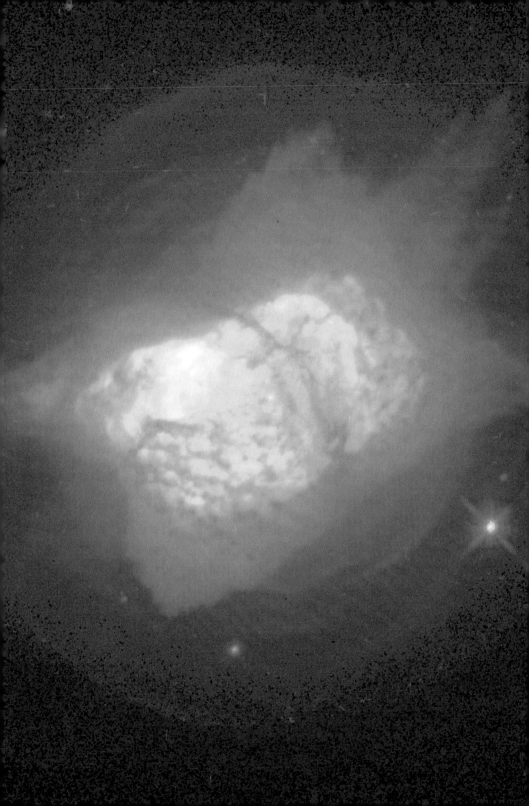

The End of the Sun

The Sun will eventually die. This will not happen for billions of years. When the Sun dies, it will create a nebula. It will become a tiny, fading star in the center of the nebula.

As the Sun uses up its fuel, it will grow to 50 times its present size. It will become cooler. Cooler stars are red. The Sun will change from yellow to red. Then it will be a giant red star.

Over time, the middle of the Sun will shrink to the size of Earth. It will become very hot and white in color. Then it will be a white dwarf star. It will blow its remaining layers of hot gas into space.

Over time, the Sun will cool off even more. It will become a black dwarf. The gas and dust in the Sun's nebula will gradually spread out into the universe.

Some of the Sun's gas will join with other nebulas. In millions or billions of years, gas from the Sun will become a new star.

Scientists believe the Sun will form a planetary nebula like this one when it dies.

Glossary

astronomer (ah-STRAHN-uh-mur)—a scientist who studies objects in space

atmosphere (AT-muhss-fear)—a layer of gases that surrounds an object in space

constellation (kon-stuh-LAY-shuhn)—a group of stars that forms a pattern in the sky

dark nebula (DARK NEB-yoo-lah)—a nebula that blocks light

emission nebula (i-MISH-uhn NEB-yoo-lah)—a nebula of very hot gases that glows from nearby starlight

fusion (FYOO-zhuhn)—the process where hydrogen atoms combine to form helium and release energy

galaxy (GAL-uhk-see)—a very large group of stars and planets

jet (JET)—a high-speed stream of very hot gas given off by new stars

nebula (NEB-yoo-lah)—a huge cloud of gas and dust in space

prism (PRIZ-uhm)—a triangle-shaped piece of glass that separates white light into its colors

reflection nebula (ri-FLEK-shuhn NEB-yoo-lah)— a nebula that reflects starlight

supernova (soo-pur-NOH-vuh)—a bright exploding star

Astronomy Picture of the Day

http://antwrp.gsfc.nasa.gov/apod/astropix.html

Future Astronauts of America

www.faahomepage.org

NASA for Kids

kids.msfc.nasa.gov

Space Telescope Institute Home Page

http://www.stsci.edu/

**Star Child: A Learning Center for
  Young Astronomers**

http://starchild.gsfc.nasa.gov/docs/StarChild/
  StarChild.html

NASA Headquarters

Washington, DC 20546-0001

Space Telescope Institute

3700 San Martin Drive
Johns Hopkins University Homewood Campus
Baltimore, MD 21218

Index